CHOOSING PEACE

One Orphan's Guide to Healing from Childhood Trauma

SHALITA O'NEALE

Disclaimer

These are my memories, from my perspective, and I have tried to represent events as faithfully as possible. I have changed some names to protect individuals' privacy.

Paperback: 978-1-7347084-0-0

First paperback edition January 2020.

Edited by CB Fletcher Creates
Cover art by Points North Design Studio

Printed by IngramSpark in the USA

Bitamalogy Publishing
9701 Apollo Drive, Suite 100
Largo, MD 20774

www.shalitaoneale.com

This book is dedicated to the little girl within me that never stopped searching for love and acceptance. Her name is Muffin.

She was not protected by those who named her. To survive the world's strife, I hid her away, the innocent girl who was ready to love. Now as a woman by many other titles and names I have returned to reclaim and embrace her. She has been hidden and her cries ignored too long. My message to her is, "I need you and you need me. You are safe here and I am safe with you. We will heal each other to break the generational curses because we need each other to love as deeply as our collective self was created to."

This is for everyone trying to reclaim and heal their connection with their inner child.

"Nothing is lost...Everything is transformed." - **Michael Ende, The NeverEnding Story**

THE JOURNEY AHEAD

NOT SUPPOSED TO BE HERE

I wasn't supposed to be here. My mother had her tubes tied before I was born, and yet I found my way to her womb. She could have terminated the pregnancy. She and my father were not in a loving relationship. In fact, they weren't in any kind of relationship because he was already in one and made it clear he wanted nothing to do with her or me. I was told by family members that when I was born, she was ready to be a mother. She was 33 years old and already had two children, my sister, and brother who are 16 and 17 years older than me respectively. She had them at a very young age when she didn't understand or want the responsibility of being a mother. I was told they suffered greatly because of that. I don't remember a lot about my mother, but I remember how it felt to be around her. Although I was very young, I remember what our bond felt like and it has remained with me until this day. I even remember how her apartment was set up. One day there was broken glass on the kitchen floor and as I was bending down to touch it, she warned me not to and swept it up. I remember watching my uncle's home videos of us at the beach and of her bathing me in the kitchen sink and loved how she interacted with me. She loved me. She spoiled me. She protected me.

When I was almost three years old my mother was stabbed 11 times and with one strike to her heart, she was taken away from me. They never brought her killer to justice, although I believe I know who killed her. After my mother's murder, I went to live with my maternal grandmother until I was 5 years old. She did her best to take care of me, but she was suffering from alcoholism and living in poverty. Trying to provide for the needs of a preschooler in that type of space was very difficult for her. When she would drink, she would become physically and verbally abusive. One of my uncles decided to take custody of me from my grandmother and I went to live with him from the age of 5 to 13 years old. Those were the most tumultuous eight years of my life. It started off smoothly. I used to call him *Uncle Daddy*. He was an extremely

5

intelligent man who knew how to do everything and was the life of the party.

They used to call him the "Jack of All Trades" because he knew how to do everything, although his main profession was corrections with Baltimore City. I used to look at him as a superhero. I think the death of my mother really affected him. I witnessed him on one occasion when I was four years old smoking something from a funny shaped glass. I now understand that what I saw was his smoking cocaine from a glass pipe.

When I was seven the physical abuse began. At times I was beaten for discipline and other times it was him working out life's frustrations on my body. The beatings would typically end with my having to soak in a bathtub of ice-cold water for about an hour. I didn't understand until I was a teenager that he had me do this to prevent me from bruising and expedite healing from the beatings. Sometimes he would tape raw meat to my bruises, and I'd sleep in it so my fair skin would not show the bruises.

One beating drove me into a mental space that no child should ever wander into. He needed a punching bag and there I stood. He would beat for a few minutes at a time and rotated his weapons of choice. Extension cord, hanger, belt, fists, the myriad of his tools were only half the horror. When I was 12, I decided that I was going to take my own life. I felt an anger rising inside of me that wanted to escape. I felt that I was either going to try to kill my uncle or he was eventually going to kill me. I thought that if I killed myself first, he wouldn't have to do it and I would no longer be a burden to him.

I was home alone and found a kitchen knife and held the sharp end against my heart, but I could not bring myself to push the knife in. I thought with one strong thrust it could all be done. That the darkness that had become my life would be replaced with the loving angelic eyes of my mother and we would dance for an eternity in heaven. No more pain, no more burdens, no more beatings, only love. I prayed often. I asked God to help me and often I felt unheard but for some reason, I felt a presence that was always with me. I could not explain it but whenever I wanted to give up or run away, it was almost as if something inside of me was reset. It was almost as if The Source allowed me to be enveloped in the strength to carry on. With tears of desperation in my eyes, I dropped the knife, fell to my knees and felt I was alive for an unknown reason and I had to keep trying.

Not long after the attempt on my life, I was beaten again until I blacked out. Afterward he stepped on my back, rubbed salt into my wounds and mouth. This beating left me with bruises that could not be covered up. Although he sent me to school the next incredibly warm day with long sleeves and pants; the bruises on my face couldn't be hidden. I had a doctor visit and she asked me where the bruises came from. I lied trying to protect my abuser and said that I had fallen off the bed and hit my face.

I thought I did a good job convincing her but in hindsight, it was clear she was aware of where they came from. I remember overhearing her say to my uncle that she had to report it. I didn't know what that meant at the time but now I know she meant she would need to make a report to Child Protective Services. After the doctor's appointment, we did not stay at home much. We spent a lot of time at the homes of his different girlfriends. Many times, he left me with them while he went about doing what he wanted to do, sometimes a day or two later.

It amazed me how much power the adults in my life had that they did not use. The teachers knew I was being beaten at home, but no one did anything. His girlfriends also knew but they also did nothing. On one occasion, I stayed the night at one of his girlfriend's houses, as I often did while he stayed at home. I was to call him in the morning to wake him up so he could come to pick me up and take me to school for a math test, but I was unsuccessful in reaching him. When I finally reached him, it was well past the time I needed to be at school. He blamed me for his being late and yelled that once I got home from school, he was going to beat me. He said it in a way that made me believe this might be the time he killed me.

I couldn't focus on class and the school day seemed to fly by. Right before the dismissal bell rang, I told one of the school administrators that I was afraid to go home because my uncle threatened to beat me badly. I had no idea what she was going to do to help me, but I hoped she would find a way to get me out of the house so that I wouldn't die by his hands. Instead, she called him and told him what I told her and sent me home. I knew for sure he was going to kill me once I got home and I didn't know where I could run away to. I had no money; I was 12 years old and didn't know anyone who would do anything other than return me to him. To my surprise, once I got home, he didn't beat me. Instead, he punished me by tearing up the tickets to a concert that I really wanted to go to. After that I lived moment to moment not knowing if he was going to change his mind and beat me.

Shortly after this incident, he sent me to Georgia to live with one of his girlfriends that I had not met but had spoken to over the phone on a couple of occasions. He told me he was going to join me at some point but never did permanently. He would only visit periodically, and I was living with her and her three children for almost a year before I convinced my uncle to let me come back to Baltimore to spend the summer with my family. I was not allowed to speak to any of my family members while I was staying with his girlfriend and when I tried to send a letter to my grandmother, he found out and beat me in front of the girlfriend I was staying with. I could tell she wanted to help me, as he lifted me up by the neck banging my head against the wall, but she didn't know how. I believe she was afraid of him too. I don't think her children liked him. They tolerated me and although they were never mean to me, I could tell I was in the way. I

11

was enrolled in a new school and was bullied and made fun of on a daily basis. I just wanted to go back to Baltimore; although there was a lot of pain there, at least I was familiar with it and that is where the only family I knew was.

My uncle ended up renting an apartment in Georgia that I would visit on the occasions he was in town. I had my own room, so I was so very excited every time I was able to be there. I thought maybe he would really move down there for good and we could start over. On one occasion, he came into town and I stayed with him at the apartment but this time instead of sleeping on my cot in my room, he had me sleep in the bed with him.

I was really uncomfortable, but I didn't have a say in whether or not I wanted to share a bed with him. It was this night that he told me that he was going to show me how to have sex. My stomach dropped and I was paralyzed. I didn't know what to do or say but the only thing I could muster was to ask him what God would think about it, since he spoke of God often. He told me that no one knew what God thought but that it was commonplace for uncles to show their nieces how to have sex. He proceeded to insert his finger into my vagina, and it hurt, and I pushed his hand away. I am thankful that he did not persist, but he promised he would soon show me how to have sex. I begged him to let me visit Baltimore for the summer because I missed my family. He protested at first with the response 'They don't care about you!'. Thankfully, shortly after this incident, we took the road trip back.

Once I was back in Baltimore, I visited with a woman who had been in a very long relationship with my other uncle ("Caesar") and who I considered to be my Aunt (I called her Aunt Kissably). I told her what had been happening to me over the years. Not only did I share about the beatings, and the recent sexual abuse but, I shared with her a repressed memory I had of my uncle molesting me when I was 3 or 4 years old.

We had just pulled up to her house after being out all day. She cut the car off and we sat there in an awkward silence as if she knew there was something I wanted to share, but she didn't want to ask. I finally broke down and told her everything and she responded that she knew for so long that something was wrong. She told me she wouldn't tell him she knew right away instead, she would ask him to let me stay with her for the summer while she thought of the best way to get me out of his custody. She did this and he agreed to let me spend the summer with her and she did as she said. She reported him and what I had been going through at his hands. She visited him one day with the intention of letting him know that she was aware of what he had done, and she was going to take me from him. When she did this he did not respond with a confirmation or declination; it was as if he knew she would eventually tell him this. He did not resist; he let me go.

After being legally removed from my uncle, I thought I was going to live with Aunt Kissably. I loved her so very much. She was the mother of four of Uncle Caesar's children and I had known her all of my life. Although they never married, I saw her as my Aunt. She was sweet and kind and understood my foster care struggle since she experienced it too. I believed I would have a better life with her, but she did not let me live with her. Instead, one of her daughters, "Tara", who was not Uncle Caesar's child and so was of no relation, decided her mother was too old to care for me and that, as a 25-year-old single mother with an 8-year-old child, would be a better option. My heart was broken. I didn't know Tara very well and I didn't know that I wanted to live with her. As she took her foster parent classes, I stayed with her and her daughter, "Kia". At the same time, there was an impending trial for the uncle that raised me for the sexual abuse I experienced with him when I was 3 or 4 years old. The Baltimore courts were unable to proceed with his case for the abuse I experienced in Georgia because it was a different state. He would have to be tried there and I knew that wasn't going to happen.

When the day of the trial arrived, I was so very sick to my stomach. It would be the first time I saw him in over a year. I was 14 years old and had to testify, detailing sexual abuse that happened to me 11-12 years prior and whose memories I had repressed. What made matters worse was my uncle was representing himself, so he cross-examined me. I had to recount what happened to me in his presence for the first time and respond to his line of questioning. I was never more terrified or hurt. I did not want him to go to jail; I wanted him to get help.

What I didn't know was prior to my testifying, he was questioned by an investigator, one-on-one, and he confessed to everything; however, he said that he would deny everything if it were to be revealed to my grandmother. The investigator realized his error at this point; he did not have a witness to these accounts in the room when my uncle was questioned. My uncle recanted and proceeded to defend himself. I also found out later that my grandmother testified against me, stating that I was a liar and had always been, in defense of her son. The jury found him not guilty and I left feeling betrayed and yet again abandoned and rejected.

When I left the courtroom all I could think was, "how could my grandmother defend him?!" If my Mom were alive, she would have believed me. Well, if my Mom was alive none of this would have happened. I never wanted to talk to her again. Not long after this heartbreak I saw the movie Soul Food and saw how the grandmother in the story died leaving a void and the family to fend for itself.

Even with how angry I was with my grandmother, I did not want her to pass away without being on speaking terms. I loved her endlessly and understood her better than anyone else. We had a connection that I would not let be broken. I finally gave in and called her. She told me she was waiting for me to call. I don't remember our making mention of the trial or what she did but, it didn't need to be said for me to know and feel that she was sorry.

A few months later she was in the hospital after a fall. She was in the hospital for a week before anyone told me she was there. By the time I found out she was in a medically induced coma to relieve brain swelling, I believe. I went to visit her and told her how much I loved her and hoped she could hear me. Ultimately, she passed away from a brain aneurysm.

I believe generational trauma is real and its effects are extremely detrimental to future generations, if left unhealed. I often wonder what my uncle's experience was like growing up to believe that treating me in such a way was acceptable. I was told he and his siblings witnessed my grandmother shoot and kill my grandfather. She told me that it was purely a mistake and I believed her, because my grandmother was not the type to lie about standing up for or protecting herself. Could it have been Karma coming back on my grandfather for beating my grandmother and having a separate family? Was my uncle punishing them through me for all the pain and trauma he experienced? There were so many questions that could only be answered by people who could no longer speak.

I had hoped for better tomorrows and was optimistic about their rise over the horizon of a bruised past. I was not supposed to be here. A little girl who came into the world to love and was met with the weight of the trauma from other people. This was my place and I had to create spaces for me to first survive and eventually thrive.

Be encouraged: Look back on your greatest pain(s) and consider that the people causing you pain were battling something you know nothing about. Can you forgive them?

PILLAR TO POST

My new day came and went within three very challenging years with Tara. Despite my new home, I suffered from major depression in transition from adolescent to teen. It was hard to balance owning my sadness and puppeteering a happy face so that I would not be heavily medicated. Although I was an honor student, worked, played volleyball, and cleaned the house enough to impress a neurosurgeon with OCD, Tara decided she could no longer parent me. I was relieved when I was removed and placed with a foster family I did not know. I thought this was my opportunity to be a part of a family that may be interested in adopting me.

This family fostered over 100 youth and were held in high regard by the foster care agency I was a ward of. I learned very quickly that my foster mother should not have been allowed to parent anyone; especially, not a child that was experiencing such turmoil. This house was a minefield of disappointments owned and operated by "Mr. and Mrs. Blue".

All I was asking for was a little freedom, but The Blues said I was not allowed to use the telephone or go into the refrigerator. All I was asking for was compassion with my depression, but Mrs. Blue ignored my pleas to stay active and instead gossiped about me to her church friends. All I was asking for was some connection to the life I could have had, but Mrs. Blue isolated me from the few family members who still loved me as their Muffin.

The Blues had another foster child living with them three years prior to my arrival. We shared a room and although she was 18, developmentally she was a 14-year-old. She began stealing money from The Blues and blamed it on me. Since they had a stronger relationship with her, the false accusation was a conviction for me. Within four months, my social worker was standing in the doorway with a clear trash bag instructing me to fill it with my belongings.

I was taken to a local group home and placed in their shelter program where I had the same restrictions as I did in my last foster home placement but only more limiting. While I was able to have my own room, I could not have visitors, use the phone, or live a normal life outside of the shelter. It was like I was being punished because I did not have parents and, up until that point, no one wanted me. Shortly after arriving, The Blues caught on to the lies of my former foster sister and removed her from their home. They invited me to come back to their home with a smile on their face. I declined.

After being at the group home's shelter for two weeks, I found out about a program they had called semi-independent living. This was my Drinking Gourd to be followed into freedom. I would get to be a teenager and live a life while still under the watchful eye of the foster care system. I expressed my interest in being considered for the program once they had an opening.

Living under the very strict and suppressive rules of my Uncle prepared me for this. It was easy for me to follow the rules of the shelter as I had lived under them all of my life. And finally, it happened! I was able to move into their semi-independent living program. Although I wanted to be adopted, the conversation never occurred with my social workers. I became used to the Group home and the staff. I forged relationships with some of the staff and had a wonderful onsite case manager and therapist that helped me identify and apply to colleges.

The group home provided for me in ways that none of my previous foster parents did. For it to be an institution, they did the best they could to normalize our experience. We would get a chance to make a Christmas list that they would grant. When I graduated from high school, they gave gifts and had a celebration for us and when it was time for me to go away to college, they purchased everything I would need as a freshman. They made sure I had a computer, printer and even shower shoes and a shower caddy. The Executive Director and I had formed a bond that I thought would last forever. It may have been an institution, but it was the closest thing to a family that I had, and I was grateful.

Over the years the Executive Director and I remained connected. He supported me through my matriculation at the University of Maryland, was a guest at my wedding in St. Lucia, and had the Group Home pay for my undergraduate loans. Although our relationship became strained for reasons I could never fully understand and we weren't able to mend the divide before his death in 2017, I will always treasure the lessons I learned from his presence in my life.

At the age of 17, I left the group home to live on campus at the University of Maryland, College Park. For the first time I had to be my own guardian without the direct support of the foster care system or parents; regardless of how much or little they contributed to my well-being. Until that point, I did not have to work, although I did, and I did not have as much freedom to govern my daily activities as when I went away to college. Technically, I was still in the foster care system, however I was still expected to operate as a functioning adult as I was not under constant supervision. I was grateful for this because I had wanted to be "on my own" since I was 15. Now was my chance.

Something may look amazing on the outside and be rotten inside. On the contrary, something may look 'meh' on the outside, but the fruit of the spirit lies within. I had to learn to be careful about what appeared as a pillar and what was indeed a post or vice versa. We do not know until we take a chance, put on a brave face and move forward with hope on the horizon.

Notes on the reflection: Follow the Drinking Gourd *was a song sung by slaves to provide directions north to freedom. The Drinking Gourd is the Big Dipper constellation.*

Journal Reflections:

◊ It's easy to look at a situation as something better than what it actually is when you are desperate. When your 'next step' is revealed as a hazardous situation, how can you navigate your way through to your Drinking Gourd?

◊ If you are unwilling to or do not have the means to seek a counselor, how do you handle your depression?

◊ What happens when you do everything that you need to in order to accomplish a goal and it does not come to fruition, such as being loved, an opportunity, or a way out? Is this a time for you to wait for someone to save yo

LAST CHANCE

Life had finally given me a clean slate to create whatever I wanted to be in my life. I dove into my full college experience as a freshman. The milk and honey of freedom that I had craved for what seemed like a lifetime was finally here and I ate it all up through every experience and my interactions. I was doing it. I was building the foundation of my own promised land and the pride of invoking the power I had in me all along to be greater. I almost flunked out in my freshman year and quickly changed my major which allowed me to bring my GPA up to an average GPA. Even with all of this, the experience was still mine. However, I didn't have any real time to process my accomplishment of making it to a University while still in foster care, because one day, I received news that I was not prepared for.

I was alone in my room preparing for a Biology exam I had in the morning and my phone rang. It was one of my cousins that I barely spoke to, but today, she had some news to give me. The Uncle, who was the closest thing I had to a father (Uncle Daddy) despite the abuse, had been shot to death in Baltimore after an attempted robbery by some strangers he gave a ride to. The room began spinning and I wailed as my heart felt like it exploded. Apparently that cousin was not supposed to share the news with me at all. The family had planned to wait until after my exams were done, come to the school, sit me down and tell me. Unfortunately, the addiction to drama drove her eagerness to spread the bad news like wildfire no matter who it hurt; she was not alone in that behavior. Despite the heartache, I had to pull it together and take my exam. I failed. I guess the failure was a blessing in disguise because biology was not my calling after all.

We laid my uncle to rest, but the family was restless all the days leading up to our final goodbye. There were all kinds of disagreements among family, with the main one being who was the beneficiary of a small policy that he held in his retirement. He had three children that I thought were surely going to receive the payout, but low and behold it was me. Me, the orphaned burden that he abused relentlessly. He used his last to send a sort of apology. I believed I was an obligation he loathed, but apparently underneath all of those demons he was fighting there was love...or guilt. Either way I was given $1,000.00. Even though in hindsight it is not enough payback for the pain (no amount would be), I **needed** that money at the time.

After six years of being removed from his custody and a few short months before his death, I had just reconnected with him as a 19-year-old college student. I thought it was my opportunity to build the relationship with him that I always wanted and help him heal from the war we had. How ironic. I wanted to heal *him*, but I was the one that needed healing. Then suddenly the chance was stolen away by two carjackers. Taken like my mother. Taken like my grandmother. Taken like my biological father who never laid claim to me.

The only one who was not taken away from a chance to heal, was me. That was a lonely and powerful place. I had to become the impossible, because I knew the price had already been paid by my elders for me to do so. They were, unfortunately, unsuited for the tasks to become more than what they were. For their lessons, despite how they came, I love and appreciate them for it. First, I had to finish college and prove everyone wrong who told me I couldn't become anything. I could see their faces in my mind when they saw me walking across the stage getting my degree. I fed off of it. I didn't stop to process my accomplishments, my pain or my feelings of isolation. I had to take care of myself. I was all I had.

Reflecting on the start of my healing transformation in 2016, I realize now that my core belief of self-care stemmed from my father abandoning me. When he found out about me, he declared he was not my father. I was unfathomably angry. I developed my own subconscious coping mechanisms to deal with my feelings. I put up an emotional barricade so no one could get close enough to disappoint or leave me ever again. Deep down, I believed I wasn't worthy of anything good because my father clearly didn't believe I was. I found out when I was 19 years old, shortly after my uncle was murdered that my father drank himself to death on a park bench three years prior. Apparently, he had a serious drinking problem for many years. I was told that he would drink before he ate in the morning. The disappointing part was that I started looking for him at 16, around the time that he died, and it was unbeknownst to me that he was taken by the bottle. When I sought out a resource at a government agency to provide his information, they stated that they could not release information on someone who is deceased, indirectly giving me the information, I needed.

It is a mantra that is beaten into our heads that life is short, and we never know when the last time will be to say I love you, forgive you, etc. With that in mind, what if this is your last chance to heal before the end? Will you waste another day being

31

angry or will you figure out how to heal from it? Generational illnesses and curses have run through my family, and perhaps this healing journey is the last chance of my bloodline to get it right and the first chance for generational blessings to begin.

Journal Reflections:

◊   Sometimes life comes at you fast and all you can do is let it hit you. Think back to a time when everything crumbled, and you found your strength to carry on. If you did it once you can do it again.

◊   What are your requirements for forgiveness? Are they legitimate or a power grab to make a person suffer as you have?

◊   Is your ambition driven by trying to prove someone wrong? That is not a bad place to start. However, if you are looking to go beyond what people said you could not do, then you must find or create an *evolving why*.

An evolving why is a goal that transforms to suit your needs as you go through life.

For example: Three Black Women were responsible for the calculations and innovation that got Americans into space. First, they needed to make sure they could get in and out of space safely. That required particular calculations and a work ethic that would create that opportunity. When it was time to go to the moon the calculations and work ethic changed to suit that opportunity. Space is space. How far you go into space is dependent on the types of work ethic and calculations that are put into it. Yet the overall goal was getting into space.

◊ Write down your ambitions and determine your why. If the reason behind the ambition cannot evolve, you are delving into a task that will not serve you in the future.

SISTA

To bring some closure to losing a father I never knew, I looked for and found my father's death certificate; unexpectedly I found something I had never had, another sister. His daughter's name appeared on the death certificate and upon more research, I found out she lived in South Carolina. Since I lost my father this could've been my opportunity to connect with his side of the family. I wrote the woman listed and mailed the letter expecting that she would not call the number I listed. She did!

When she and I spoke, my dream of finally being connected to family seemed to be possible. I felt like we were about to reunite like Celie and Netti and bond like Celie and Shug Avery in *The Color Purple*; because of that fantasy, I'll call her *"Sista"*. I found out she was 10 years older than me and had a two-year-old child. She was nice and seemed to be excited to hear from me. We spoke about getting a DNA test to be 100% sure because she had been told by our father that I was not his child. Every time we spoke about my father, out of respect, I never called him my father. I would say "your father" because I truly began to question the story, I heard from my family about him being my father and until I was 100% sure, I didn't want to disrespect my sister.

Sista asked me if there was anything special about my eyes, because my father had distinct eyelids and that she had them too as it was something that ran in the family. After I sent her a photo of me, Sista called me crying, because as the picture loaded it froze under my eyes and she knew I was her sister even without a DNA test. At this point, we began to talk about what our father had shared with her about my mother and I. Sista said she was disappointed because she always wanted a little sister.

Sista told me that our father told her that a paternity test was taken, and it was determined I was not his child. Back in the 80s you couldn't just ask for a paternity test or spit in a cup like we do today.

A court order needed to be filed for custody and as part of that process a DNA test was administered. At that time the tests were stored in the Archives in Baltimore City. I explained to her that when I searched in the Archives myself, my parents' names were not there; therefore, he never took a paternity test. It was at the moment she realized he lied to her. Once I told her this, she stopped all communication with me.

One more rejection. One more love lost. I was so close! Yet the cinematic reunification I had imagined in my mind dissipated when Daddy's little girl, Sista, learned of his dark side or maybe she was always aware and this news and our inability to connect until now was another disappointment my father was responsible for in her life that she had to now deal with after his death. I could've had a loving relationship with the closest person to my biological father. Even she did not feel I was worth trying to build a relationship with, *like father, like daughter*. I turned to drinking to mask my worthlessness. The irony was I preferred dark liquor just like my father and we had never met. I would drink a pint of Christian Brothers every night until I fell asleep and kept moving forward. I didn't stop to process how this made me feel or how it tied in with how my father's absence affected me. It was just another event that happened in my life that was evidence I did not matter, and I was not worthy of love.

Journal Reflections:

◊ It's not always about you. People will come into and leave your life for different reasons. Our first instinct is to internalize their inability to stay.

◊ Blood isn't thicker than water. Being related to someone by blood does not guarantee their participation in your life.

IT'S ALL ABOUT WHO YOU KNOW

The rest of my college experience was a challenge. When I told people that I wanted to be a Forensic Pathologist because dissecting crime scenes and even bodies to solve a case, they would be shocked and accuse me of being morbid. Some people said it was probably because of my mother's death that I was so interested in crime scene investigation; especially *since her killer was never brought to justice.* As I think about it, maybe they were right but Forensic Pathology or at least the biology and chemistry components were not my strong suit.

When I graduated high school, I was in the top 10% of my class, but my teachers did not really push or educate me in a way that would have prepared me for a pre-med major in college. I decided to change my major to Criminology and Criminal Justice, in my sophomore year, as this was still a part of what I wanted to do. This was the first time I was on the Dean's List in college and I ended up graduating without destroying my GPA.

Later I learned that most college students don't end up working in the fields they studied, but it didn't matter, I did it! I graduated from college, the first in my family! With all the excitement I had about reaching that first major life milestone, I did not celebrate. I felt this looming haunting force over me. It felt as if I turned the corner, I would be facing this being that was out to destroy me, so I ran from it. I allowed this force to chase me into a corner where I could not stop and celebrate and where I could not enjoy the moment. It was a mental manifestation of the fear of failure and not proving those naysayers wrong, especially my father but, I used the fear to propel me towards finding my true destiny and source of my life's passion.

After graduating, I realized that a degree did not mean I would be employed in the career of my choosing. I learned that it was about who you knew, not your resume, that gets you employed. I didn't know anyone in the FBI or in any career path that would allow me to use my criminology degree, so I went to work in retail. I was the co-manager for a

39

women's clothing store for three years before I had a nervous breakdown. This was not my calling and I wasn't quite sure what my calling was, which frustrated me even more. *'Where do I fit?'* I asked myself. I've been out of place my whole life, *where do I go so, I don't suffocate here?*

One day, I was connected to a woman who was the Executive Director of an organization that helped foster youth participate in the performing arts. She recruited me to raise funds for the organization on a volunteer basis and that evolved into me becoming the Marketing Director for two years. I had a chance to connect with young people in foster care one-on-one and within that experience, I discovered my calling. It was to change the outcomes of foster youth one by one and collectively.

I would listen to their stories and witness what they were going through in foster care; many of the same situations I experienced. This birthed the idea to start a non-profit organization to help them navigate life after foster care because so many of them did not get adopted and left the foster care system at the age of 18 or 21 without support. My focus shifted from outrunning failure to creating opportunities for young people who were leaving the foster care system without a clue on how to survive in the real world. I went to school to dissect crime scenes and ended up dissecting every issue within the foster care experience and using it to make a change. The degree was never a waste of time.

Journal Reflections:

◊ When you put more energy into running from your fears, you will manifest mental roadblocks that keep you from your desires.

◊ Think about the last time you asked yourself, am I qualified on a mental, emotional, and spiritual level to be in the circumstance that I am in? If the answer is yes, continue to grow in that space. If the answer is no, start asking about/meditating on where you are supposed to be.

Be encouraged: If you have hit a dead end in your career, embrace the prospect of finding your calling and what you need to fulfill that calling will start showing up in ways you never imagined.

DON'T WRECK YOUR FUTURE, RUNNING FROM YOUR PAST

When you've endured something painful, you cannot see the reason for it. Until, you must conjure the strength you gained from that experience and use it to change your future.

This is Sankofa.

I considered myself superior to my former life, however, the way I was living to prove that superiority was ultimately inferior to the woman that I was meant to become. Running that "escape the doom" road until my feet bled felt like the right way to do it, but it did not serve my soul. Trying to prove yourself can become a lifestyle if you let it, but you will never rest. If the root of your power is your pain, your *'superiority'* or *'I made it, now what!'* mantra is inferior to who you are meant to be.

My determination brought me to a place in my life where I achieved far more than most people my age or from my background. However, I had to constantly remind myself to appreciate and enjoy my accomplishments at the moment. Everything that happened to me was driving my determination to be the greatest. Unfortunately, creating faux superiority is a pattern that repeats with traumatized people and it puts future success at risk by seeking materialistic wealth that is fleeting, disregarding present blessings in exchange for what is yearned, losing self in the midst of over loving, and reducing worth to uncharted lows to impress dysfunctional people.

After experiencing faux superiority, I learned that life is not a race. It is important to stop and appreciate accomplishments and the good things in life. Stop trying to please others or be accepted by people who do not acknowledge your worth. To do so, you must acknowledge your worth. Stop seeking validation from others and accept it from yourself. If you don't believe you are worthy, no one else will.

Life is not about fighting for things that already belong to you. Stop fighting against the greatness that is inside you and tap into it. When you do, you will have absolutely nothing to prove.

When you try to pursue love and acceptance from those who have discounted you, it is because their approval coddles your rage that empowers your faux superiority. In turn, the anointed people chosen to bring joy, peace, comfort, and/or success into your life are pushed out, because they have accepted you for who they are in journey, and 'that person' they love is not loved by you. Ultimately, what are you trying to prove to yourself when everyone else can see how great you are?

I've learned that the family I've made for myself is all I really need. I don't need acceptance or love from people that have never been present for praises or pitfalls. Leave the past where it is, in the past. Take a breath and take in your present. Hold your children, your partner and your best friends close to you. Release toxic people and situations. Recognize your dreams and aspirations and know that you can and will reach them in your own time. You have made it through some of the worst set of circumstances. The worst is behind you. Anything calling itself tough will pale in comparison to what you've been through.

Stop running. Right now, at this moment, you are right where you need to be.

Journal Reflections:

◊ What/who are you struggling to let go of or forgive?

◊ Why are you having a hard time forgiving?

◊ What in your past are you running from? Why?

◊ Is refusing to forgive working for you?

◊ What is refusing to forgive costing you? Is it worth the price?

◊ What will you do differently to release the hold unforgiveness has on your life?

◊ How will you begin to show yourself compassion?

◊ How will you begin to forgive yourself?

FINDING LOVE

I did not know if I was ever going to find someone who truly unconditionally loved me for who I was. I had been in a couple of serious relationships before I met the man who would become my husband. We met in college. He was a senior and I was a junior and somehow, we had the same circle of friends. When we met, I had just ended a 4-year relationship with my high school sweetheart. I missed out on being *free* during most of my college experience because I was dedicated and reserved for him. After we split, I promised myself that I was going to sew my wild oats and enjoy the rest of my college experience.

Then, I met Brian and that was out the window. We clicked in a way that I had never experienced before. He was a drop-dead, heart-stopping, foot-stomping, call your girlfriend so she can witness this beautiful sexy being. As I got to know him, I found his true beauty was in his intelligent and philosophical mind, old soul and kind heart. He showed me how loyal and loving he was by how he treated his mother. He was not clingy to her, but he made time for her. I had not witnessed a man treating his mother that way. Brian embodied the phrase "the way a man treats his mother is the way he'll treat his wife."

So, 4 years, an island engagement and a wedding later, I had found love in a safe place. Finally.

However, we had to create that safe place. The door was created but we needed to build a house around it. I was bringing in my baggage from my childhood and he had baggage of his own. People have asked how I allowed someone to love me, given what I had been through. It required us both to be willing to unpack together.

I was so used to providing for myself and being an *independent woman.* Having to confer with someone else about my plans, my finances, or anything else was foreign to me. When I released my anxiety of proving myself as a "solo act" and accepted support I felt relieved. There was finally room to build myself up instead of running away from this idea that I was never good enough. While this is still a work in progress, it wasn't until I began to unpack where these feelings came from and why I built up such a belief system around the need to be independent. This belief came from feeling like a burden to everyone as a child, so I promised myself that I would never be a burden again. If I didn't make things happen for myself, no one else would because they wouldn't believe I was worthy of it. The truth was, I didn't believe I was worthy of it.

Working through my fear of abandonment, rejection, and conflict resolution without cutting someone off was a worthy battle. My defense mechanism was to remove people from my life at the first sign of discourse. I wanted to protect myself from the rejection I experienced when my father disowned me. My husband unpacked my fears and turned them into tools of healing and balance by showing me that disagreement did not mean being unloved. He demonstrated that it was alright to depend on someone other than myself by being an asset to my endeavors and my healing journey.

When we were newlywed, I left my full-time job to pursue a dream of creating an organization for foster youth in 2008, The Maryland Foster Youth Resource Center (MFYRC). My husband willingly supported our household because he believed in my vision, although I was not making an income at the time. He and I have been rocking for 17 years so far while toting our young son on this journey. I'm grateful for this marriage so that the cycle of abuse and trauma can end, and our son can live with a clean slate on a foundation of love. My own separate journey of love came through my first vision, The MFYRC.

The organization eventually became Hope Forward in 2015. It provided transitioning foster youth with life skills, resources, and long-term solutions to create systems change through leadership and advocacy. It was acquired by a larger organization in 2016 and I hoped the services we provided would continue well into the future, but they closed the program in 2017. I knew it was a possibility that the organization would be dismantled, but the next move was already in progress.

In 2012, I founded the Fostering Change Network LLC. I was working on this organization on a part time basis, while running Hope Forward. Although I wanted to dive into it more, the timing was off. When Hope Forward was acquired I took it as a sign to move on. Fostering Change Network LLC provides technical assistance to child welfare agencies and organizations looking to develop and improve programming for young adults in and from foster care. We also provided personal and professional development to young adults from the foster care system through our annual Alumni Powerhouse Networking Conferences, which was a mission ultimately adapted by the Fostering Change Network Foundation, established in 2017. The purpose was based upon my experience of coming out of college being dismayed by my potential failure.

As I made this transition, it became apparent that to go to the next level, I would need to be different. The story of foster care that had allowed me to be successful with Hope Forward was no longer who I was. Being a foster youth is still a part of my story, although I am no longer living within that chapter of my life. In 2016, a friend introduced me to Momentum Education, a prominent organization, known for providing quality results driven coaching, dynamic personal development workshops and highly experiential team building and professional development courses. When I had an experience with this organization it allowed me to see the power, I had in creating my own reality. I was ready to move from one major accomplishment to another without processing what has worked and what hasn't worked over the past 23 years.

To realize my vision, I had to choose to believe differently, think strategically, act intricately, and be open to possibilities. I had to be different than the woman that trauma raised. My vision was to create a space where people realized their full potential and manifest from it. Additionally, I wanted to build a support system that will help foster children and alumni of foster care obtain physical, mental, emotional, financial and spiritual wealth. If this were to be birthed from me, the space for it to cultivate had to be created within myself first and then the vision would manifest itself.

When you're moving so fast trying to fix all the broken pieces in your life, you miss celebrating the victories in between. It wasn't until I started to see what the future could become that I finally allowed myself to praise the progress. I fell in love, a purpose was revealed, and paths were created because I gave the universe a chance to nurture me and use my experience to cultivate a safe space for myself and all those I love.

Journal Reflections:

◊ What victories have you had through your path that are worth celebrating? Have you found your safe space within yourself to allow love to grow there?

◊ Everyone has baggage. Don't turn away love for the sake of protecting yourself with the faux armor you have created from your baggage. That does more harm than good. Unpacking those bags of trauma is a gift to yourself and to the person who is willing to love you for who you were, are, and can become.

◊ Trying to do "it" all alone is a fool's errand. *It* may be a project. *It* may be a healing journey. *It* may be a company. But you never will do *it* all alone. So, stop trying to! Accept help in being your incredible self.

◊ Where you start is not where you will finish. Just because you have one vision does not mean it will not evolve into something else. Allow yourself to be flexible in how life course winds and the possibilities will be endless.

LET THAT SHIT GO

It's been said that holding hate in your heart towards another person is like clenching on to a hot stone and burning yourself before you throw it at your enemy. I've endured betrayal and built-up hate in my heart through the years, regardless if it was with family, friends, or lovers. All the resentment that I thought was my fuel to conquer the impossible, was actually burning up my chances to have inner peace. Everyone has their own personal process of forgiveness, however, when you discover that the rage you held onto no longer serves its 'purpose' you must learn how to **let that shit go**.

Let yourself come to a place of reassessment. Dive deeper beyond the rage to dissect why a person has wronged you or why you feel they have wronged you. Create the narrative from an objective perspective that will explain the rationale behind the person's actions and how you feel about it.

That shit is going to hurt your ego, because

when we develop rage against someone, we feel justified and powerful in our stance on the matter without reassessing the situation. We go through a process similar to grieving that includes shock of the betrayal, confusion, anger over the confusion and betrayal, sadness while assessing the action and becoming enraged again, and finally accepting your hate towards the person.

Go forward and decide to heal. Understand that the person's actions stemmed from a sickness and/or pain that they were suffering from and they unleashed it onto you for some reprieve. Forgiveness is for you. You may never receive an apology from those that have wronged you because they may not even be sorry. When you make the choice to drop that hot stone of vengeance and hate and recreate a narrative of healing, you take back the power you have given those who have wronged you.

They didn't know what else to do.

Because of my father's absence I battled with rejection and inadequacy. I took it very personally that he did not want to be in my life. When I found out about his death, my pinned-up rage was from a combination of him choosing not to be in my life and never being granted the chance to get closure. I could not tell him how his absence made me feel. I could no longer hope for a happy reunion. I found out that he had a severe drinking problem and was better off without him. Even if he considered coming back for me, he could've brought more pain to my life than a life without him. I choose to believe The Universe/God knew the demons he was battling would latch onto me and kept him away to spare my future. By witnessing the love my husband has for our son, I am able to replenish what was taken from me. I had to learn to be content never knowing what my father actually thought, but knowing I have the ability to ensure my child's experience would not mirror my own.

They knew, and they didn't care.

I believe my sister killed my mother and I had to forgive her. For years the speculation was that my father killed her, possibly due to her disrupting his life with news of me and trying to hold him accountable when he was already in a relationship. To this day my sister claims her innocence in the matter, since she *discovered* my mother's body in a pool of blood. However, per the family's whispers and evidence provided by the detective over my mother's cold case, their volatile relationship and physical altercations would suggest otherwise. She refused to take a lie detector test and provided her version of events that did not support the evidence found, furthering her guilt. My sister is the one who called me *Muffin*, so how could I hate her? I didn't want to hate her but, at one point I did because she was the reason I would never get to experience my mother for myself. After A LOT of unpacking, I made the choice to release the hate and disappointment I had for her action.

Holding onto it would not bring my mother back and would always work against my better interests. I chose forgiveness because this generational pain must not be passed on to our children. I pray that my sister will be able to forgive herself and heal. That is the only thing that can set things right for my sister, for our family and for her children.

It's not their fault, it's the circumstances.

I had to forgive my mother. It's absurd to think that I was actually upset with her for dying! I was upset that she died and left me alone. It was always embarrassing when there were family functions at school and everyone else had their mother there and instead my grandmother or uncle accompanied me – if they accompanied me at all. I missed my mother during my milestones and while it was not her fault for being dead, I wanted an explanation for her absence. One day I found peace through having compassion as a mother myself and sympathizing with the pain of being away from my child when it is out of my control. Every day I look at my son, hold him in my arms and watch him grow, I am comforted in knowing that if my mother felt about me the way I feel about him, I was truly loved.

The forgiveness starts from within.

The interpretation of situation and people are the cause of personal discomfort and unhappiness, not necessarily the circumstances themselves. Those interpretations are in direct correlation with what you truly feel about yourself based on how you interpreted the actions of someone you trusted. Before you can **let that shit go**, you must look inward and develop a perspective grounded in why the circumstance affected you the way it did. This is the process of forgiving yourself. My process looked something like this:

Love thy self.

As a child, I desperately wanted to be accepted by a family because I felt I was not accepted by my own. I believed that if I did everything a family would want, I would be liked and accepted which translated into my becoming a perfectionist and control freak. The problem with this is my idea of perfection was unnecessary and unattainable. I was constantly disappointed when the families I stayed with did not embrace me the way I wanted them to. Their disapproval drove nasty internalized thoughts of myself that were more abhorrent than anything anyone else could have thought of me. Understanding that compelled me to create my own shield of love and change my internal conversation about myself.

When I realized that I was my own shield, I had to forgive the fact I hadn't put it up before. By embracing my unique self, not only do I attract the types of people I want in my life, but also, I give silent permission for others to do the same. I had to create my shield of love and confidence by spending quality time with myself, doing things I like to do even if it is sitting quietly without distractions from modern technology. I've created a room in my home that I call the Vision Room, which is a space all my own, full of affirmations on my chalkboard wall, fun colors, candles, incense and plants.

What does this look like for you? Do you make time for yourself? Have you pursued the things that interest you despite what others say? Do you date yourself? You know, take yourself out to dinner and a movie for no apparent reason. Do you look at yourself in the mirror every day and tell yourself how beautiful and amazing you are? If not, start there.

No matter how egregious the offense, you have the power to reclaim your memories, your now and your future. There comes a time when we can no longer blame others for our pain, especially when we are conscious of why we're feeling the pain. You have to do the work and it is a process, but it is a process that we all get to steer.

If you do not forgive yourself and show yourself compassion first, you cannot expect it from anyone else. Embrace who you are without the fear of rejection from anyone.

Journal Reflections:

◊ Can you forgive someone that is a victim of their circumstances?

◊ Will you forgive someone who is not sorry for what they have done for the sake of your own peace?

◊ Write down mistakes that you need to make amends for, even if it is just with yourself.

◊ Let that shit go. Follow the steps and write down things people have done to you, categorize them, and write a letter or statement to that person.

BE TRUSTING

To get you must give. This includes giving your trust in another person in order for them to trust you in the same way.

After being on a journey of self-exploration, I have to admit that I never really trusted anyone. Absolutely no one. I trusted my ability to bounce back if and when they disappointed me. I've done it countless times and I always come back stronger than before. But this journey has shined a light on the consequences I've experienced as a result of my never truly trusting anyone.

Many people have asked me how I learned to trust people when they had consistently disappointed and abused me all my life. As a child, most people I encountered were not worthy of my trust. The ones I allowed the most influence over my feelings and how I perceived myself in this world were my mother, biological father, and my youngest uncle. My mother earned my trust starting while I was in the womb. For almost three years, I could count on her to provide everything I needed with tremendous love and care until she was taken away from me. As a child, I could not understand why she was gone.

The day she was murdered was my first day of daycare. One of the daycare providers had to sit with me well after the daycare closed until someone could come and pick me up. Finally, one of my uncles came to get me. I don't recall sitting on the front steps of the daycare with the teacher, but I can imagine I knew something was wrong and wondered where my mommy was. She was gone and I did not understand how my best friend would abandon me like this; my trust was shattered. That moment taught me that even when people have the best intentions, they will still disappoint you and sometimes they're not to blame but it doesn't hurt any less.

Because of my father's absence, and subsequent abuse and molestation from one of my uncles, my trust in any man that would enter my life was destroyed. While living with my uncle, I could not trust that my basic needs would be met consistently without my having to figure out a way to make sure they were. There were times our water and electricity were cut off, there wasn't any food in the house and when he did not show up to school events that mattered to me. I had no father and no home. I had a place to stay. I had an adult present. I had some needs met. Yet, it was a toxic environment and lifestyle that no trust could settle in.

I have consistently and in quick concession lost everyone I have ever loved or cared about as a child to death. My Mother at age 2, my Aunt at age 7, my great-grandmother at age 10, my grandmother at age 14, my biological father at 16, my uncle with whom I lived with at age 19, my cousin and one of my best friends at age 29 and my favorite uncle at age 33. For all intent and purposes, I concluded that people couldn't be trusted beyond the point I could pick myself up from their betrayal.

There is a price to pay for refusing to trust wholeheartedly and it infests every part of our life. It is never truly being able to trust yourself because you don't give it to others. It is never truly being able to embrace and love yourself because you don't trust others with yourself. It is always hiding in plain sight to avoid disappointment and betrayal. It is having a false sense of control over situations that challenge your belief in yourself. It is failing to see the beauty and love in others because you don't want to look too hard, fearing you will be seen. Refusing to trust others doesn't protect you; it opens you up to the type of self-inflicted turmoil that hurts worse than someone else breaking your trust. There is no greater pain than the pain that comes from refusing to trust, accept and love yourself.

I didn't notice just how untrusting I was until I started doing the work of unpacking and analyzing myself. I realized that I had never truly and completely opened up and revealed all of myself to myself, let alone my husband, son and others that I care about so much. You would think that as much as I thought I trusted myself, that I would have at least been open and honest with myself about who I was, what I wanted out of life and how I maybe helping or hurting myself in achieving it. I was so busy running from my past and trying to prove the naysayers wrong that I neglected getting to know my true self, what she liked to do and what made her happy. Once I realized what these things were, I made it a point to pursue them, even at the risk of everything else falling apart around me.

Shortly after enrolling in Momentum Education, I decided I was going to resign from the organization I had started eight years prior, which had been acquired by a larger organization out of New York. I was tired. Tired of fighting to raise funds for the organization, tired of the politics involved with growing a nonprofit organization, tired of being responsible for the livelihood of others and tired of running from the responsibility of self-reflection. I was mentally, physically and emotionally tired. I knew what I needed to do but I was afraid. I was afraid of what other people would think of me and the organization that I had built, which was an extension of me. I had already experienced situations where people questioned my leadership and credibility without merit; I just knew leaving my organization would be the end of me. I had to take time to pick apart this fear and call it out for what it was – a story that I had made up in my mind, that I was having an adverse reaction to.

I asked myself (void of emotion and without making it about me), "What is the worst that could happen?" and "If that happens, what does it truly mean and how will you deal with it?"

The answers were:

The worst that could happen is the organization would cease operations and everyone employed by the organization would have to move on. There wouldn't be another organization in the state that did what we did for former foster youth, which will leave a gap in resources for them. I'll have to release the illusion of having control of the viability of my organization regardless of the outcome. For the first time in my life, I had to choose me. Whatever happened as a consequence of choosing myself, was worth it.

I resigned on July 14, 2016 and the organization closed its doors in the summer of 2017. When I resigned, I felt like a weight was lifted off of my shoulders. I felt a release that I did not anticipate. Deep within my being, I knew I had made the right choice. However, that choice and how I made it did not come without consequence. I resigned with only one consulting contract lined up for my LLC. I earned more money from that two-day consulting contract than I did from a month of working with my Nonprofit and I made the mistake of thinking it would always be like that. Well, I didn't have any other contracts lined up after that one and when I was unable to contribute financially to my household not only did I begin to panic but, it began to uncover deep-seated issues with my relationship with money. I left a steady paycheck for a career of uncertainty and I was beginning to question if I made the right choice.

I'm here to tell you that when you begin to break the vicious cycle of your negative thought patterns, other detrimental behaviors will make themselves known. When you truly make the decision to go inward and unpack the behaviors and actions that no longer serve you, that is your bold message to The Universe that you are ready to see and confront that which you have avoided for so long. You must steady yourself for what you will experience and know that at first, it will feel like you are being attacked but once you realize that it is what you asked for, and you asked for it with a clear head and pure heart, you will gain a confidence to keep moving forward that you did not know lived inside of you. Trust it. Trust Yourself.

Just when I felt the release of burden and excitement of being able to explore what I truly wanted by resigning from the organization I birthed, I was hit with a financial shitstorm that brought me to my knees and showed me how unresolved trauma was manifesting in my finances. It unveiled my communication issues with my husband, the void I

73

was trying to fill with materialistic possessions and my subconscious attitude about money versus my conscious attitude.

I went into what I thought was a downward spiral and a very dark place. It was in this place that I was able to truly see my situation for what it was. I was able to listen to the people around me, namely my husband, in a way that I had been unwilling to in the past. I had gotten to a point where I needed to completely depend on my husband. I did not realize that for the entire time we had been together, I had demasculinized him in many ways with my "Independent Woman Attitude". I did not allow him to truly be there for me because I wouldn't even tell him when I was in a tough spot financially until the consequences were unavoidable. I didn't communicate well in any aspect. I didn't even share when I was sad about something or honor my feelings about past traumas that would show up unexpectedly. I felt I needed to protect him from my "issues" and in doing so, I was actually alienating him. For someone who deeply appreciates

74

transparency and consistent communication, I was not giving it. I wasn't giving it to my husband, and I wasn't giving it in my long-standing friendships.

I made the decision to humble myself and listen to those closest to me that truly loved me and had stood by me even when I was behaving in a way that was unlovable. I let my guard down and listened. When was the last time you let your guard down, listened to and trusted yourself and your loved ones? It was uncomfortable to put it politely, but I told The Universe/Source/God that I wanted to reach a different level in my life, and I was committed to doing the work to attain it.

I began to change small behaviors like calling while I was out for more than a few hours to let my husband know that I was okay and before spending money from our joint account, checking in to make sure it wouldn't affect the payment of a bill or other plans. It sounds small and insignificant but those "courtesies" showed my husband that I cared about us as a Unit and that I cared about our joint aspirations. It made him want to go out of his way to show his appreciation; it made him feel respected as a man and my partner. It made him trust my word. I didn't understand until that point that my actions prevented him from trusting my word.

Once I began to see how my actions, that stemmed from my childhood trauma, were affecting relationships in my adulthood, I felt so foolish. I was ashamed that I could behave in such a way that jeopardized the well-being of my family. It was at this point that I also needed to learn to forgive myself. I had to show myself compassion, understanding that I did the best I could with what I knew. The defense mechanisms I developed as a child were severely flawed and raggedy. They got me through some horrible situations as a child, but those same defense mechanisms were not able to support me in the next part of my life where I wanted to do more than survive.

If you want to thrive instead of merely surviving, you must be open to exploring new ways of living. More likely than not, if you don't trust others, you have proven yourself to be untrustworthy in some way. You get to explore this and determine what you will do differently to create a life where you give and receive trust freely without fear of being harmed or doing harm.

Journal Reflections:

◊ What does Trust look like to you?

◊ How does your lack of trust for others show up in your life? What has it cost you?

◊ What are some ways that YOU have proven to be untrustworthy? How can you change this?

◊ How are you projecting lack of trust onto others?

KNOW YOUR WORTH

Worth is measured by your own self love and the willingness to grow beyond your worst fears and negative influences.

It may seem unbelievable, but how we view the world is shaped by our views and relationships (or lack thereof) with our parents. This is a bit *Freudian,* however that theory is on point! A child's first lessons with social interactions and norms come from their parent(s) and immediate family members. Many of these lessons are not actively taught, we learn them through our observations and internal explanations and representations of those closest to us. For instance, a child that witnesses their mother being beaten by their father and their father subsequently leaving or being ousted from the home may interpret his leaving as being their fault. While illogical, as a young child whose entire world is centered around them, witnessing such things contributes to the establishment of self-worth.

Why then, do we carry this thinking into our adulthood and allow it to guide what we believe we deserve? Again, it makes no logical sense, but emotion is not rational and that is where most of us operate from. Emotion. I realized that as an adult, I was looking at everyone and everything through the lens of UNs:

Unwanted | I was not worthy of love.

Unlovable | If my father did not love me, no one would and should.

Unprotected | Since my father did not protect me, no one could, and I should not allow anyone to try.

Untrustworthy | I should not allow anyone to get close enough to me to hurt me like my father did.

Unselfish | I should aim to be likeable by putting others before myself to prevent people from leaving me like my father.

This lens dangerously governed every relationship I ever had with anyone, especially myself. Something that continues to baffle me is how I treated myself based on all of these beliefs. We don't understand that our relationship with others is a direct mirror of the relationship we have with ourselves and the relationship we have with ourselves is in direct connection to the relationship we had or wish we had with our parent(s).

Let me go a little further by turning the statement about to "I" statements:

1. I was not worthy of loving myself.

2. If my father did not love me, I wouldn't and shouldn't.

3. Since my father did not protect me, I cannot.

4. I should not allow myself to get close to myself as I may hurt myself the way my father did.

5. I should aim to be likeable so that I will not abandon myself or grow to hate myself, as I believe my father did.

I did not begin to learn to love myself until a few years ago. There is such a thing as divine timing, and when I was introduced to the Momentum Education program I was in a transitional space where the unhealthy life practices nurtured by toxic beliefs would no longer serve me, so I had to heal if I was going to grow as both a woman and professional. The program gave me space to analyze where my beliefs truly originated.

As a result of my outdated and false beliefs, I did not truly take the time to get to know or appreciate myself. I approached everything from a place of fear. I am afraid of heights, deep water, bees and other insects and I have weird phobias that I am working to challenge. All in an effort to protect myself from the unknown. Since I never knew what it was really like to be protected due to the absence of both my parents, I kept myself safe from the unknown by avoiding it through evasion. I stayed busy to avoid being still enough to sit with my issues because, I knew that if I did, I would drive myself into a place of despair. To shield myself from possible outside attacks or my own psyche, I developed a fierceness that seemingly protected me from being taken advantage of. At times it manifested as a need to defend myself even when it wasn't necessary. Deep down inside, I didn't even believe I could do this...any of it.

I strived to be liked by everyone even though I did not like myself. I found issues with my body, my looks, my personality and my feelings. I did not like any of these things about myself. I had never been the truest version of myself because I refused to embrace every part of me, even the short-tempered, vengeful and violent part of me. Don't misunderstand, I am naturally a "happy go lucky", loving and outgoing person, but I often exaggerated this part of me to make up for the dark part of me. I used the same standards of likeability on myself as I did with others. Those standards were to always be smiling, never gripe about my situation, put the needs of others first and to learn what other people like and do that. **Denying any part of yourself is denying all of who you are.** Even the most dark and desolate parts of you deserve to be loved and sometimes the very parts we label as dark and desolate aren't truly dark and desolate at all. We misunderstand ourselves often because we are using the labels created by others (who do not like themselves) to understand our own light and dark inner workings.

We are all divine beings from the moment we come into this world. You don't have to earn your divinity. However, many of us end up having to reclaim or find it later on in life because from early on we are constantly told how unworthy and wretched we are by society, some of our religious institutions and other people who have lost their understanding of who they truly are. You are worthy of everything good, loving and sacred, no matter what anyone says.

I certainly am still on a journey of self-acceptance and understanding my worth. I use affirmations to remind myself of just how beautiful I am, inside and out. I post them around my home in spaces where I spend the most time or tend to go often like the bathroom mirror, my dresser mirror, on the chalkboard wall in my Vision Room and in my journal. The interesting thing about affirmations is they don't have to be true in the moment to manifest. Before Michael Jordan was one of the (if not THE) best basketball players alive, he said that he was even when he was cut from his high school varsity team.

Your thoughts become words. Your words become actions and your actions create your reality. Make sure you are spending more time on positive thoughts of affirmation than the negative because what you think about most is what you will see more of. Have you ever met someone that had only negative things to say? They were always complaining about their situation and it seemed they never ran out of things to gripe about? It also seemed that only negative things continued to happen to them. That is because that is what they focused on all of the time.

We all go to dark spaces. We all have toxic traits. We also all have the ability to develop our own self-worth through what we choose to think, believe, develop, act upon, and ultimately thrive in. You have a choice to feed your fear or your faith; the one you feed will grow and become your reality. Start with:

I AM WORTHY.

Chapter Notes: Sigmund Freud was an Austrian neurologist that created the practice of psychoanalysis and birthed the Freudian theory which is: The unconscious mind governs behavior to a greater degree than people suspect.

Empowerment Activity: On sticky pads write down 10 things you love about yourself and 10 things you

85

want for yourself (no matter how unrealistic you think they are) and post them in places where you will see them often. Imagine yourself having the things you want for yourself. Take a moment to love on yourself and admire the 10 things you like about yourself. Just by doing this, if only for a moment you shift your energy to that which is in line with what you truly want for yourself and those you care about.

BE UNAPOLOGETICALLY IN LOVE WITH YOURSELF

You are a star, you are the moon, you are the sun, you are your own universe and it's beautiful; treat yourself as such.

Although many of us agree that love is life, love is stronger than hate and love can overcome all barriers, we have a difficult time loving ourselves. At every turn, we are given reasons to dislike ourselves. As women, we are fed unrealistic and unrelatable standards of beauty in the media, from family members and institutions/businesses where we work and patron. As a Black Woman, I was raised to believe that I was inferior to White people and especially White Women. I was raised to dislike my natural hair, my "Ebonics", and my skin color. I remember wanting light eyes and running around the house with a towel on my head, pretending it was long flowing hair. My grandmother used to tell me that if I ate my carrots, I would have pretty eyes. I thought that meant I would wake up one day with green or blue eyes. It wasn't until later on in my adult years that I learned carrots improve vision, not the color of your eyes. Those small seeds of self-hatred planted early on that grow into poisonous thoughts and behaviors that seem impossible to shake.

'You are bright. You are intelligent. You are articulate!', strangers would say to me but, these very things were shamed by my grandmother in her drunkenness. I looked at the world through very innocent eyes. I wanted to see the best in everyone and everything. My grandmother used to fuss at me because I would sit on the front porch and speak to everyone that passed by. She would tell me not to speak to people that I didn't know or one day one of them would kidnap me. As a mother now, I understand her fear and her need to protect me from harm but at the time I didn't understand. Despite the harsh delivery of her protection, there were still many contributing factors to not loving myself as a child.

When I went to live with my *Uncle Daddy* at the age of five, the lead up to me living with him was as tumultuous as it was living with them for the eight years that I did. There was a custody battle and ego war about who could be the better parent; although both ultimately were abusive. Uncle Daddy had better income due to his Jack of All Trades work ethic, but his love ethic lacked the same energy. In addition to the beatings he unleashed on me, he unintentionally taught me how to devalue myself. I witnessed how he manifested his own belief that women were not as intelligent as men and dating multiple women was just how it was done. He didn't value me, he couldn't, because he too could not value himself.

I wanted to be rescued from this prison of self-hate and so with a pillowcase full of clothes I was ready to run away at the age of 9, but my fear of the unknown kept me locked in that place. My older brother would come to visit from Oregon periodically and I would beg him to take me with him when he was leaving, but he couldn't. Although he was 16 years my senior, he wasn't stable financially or emotionally due to our mother's murder.

The courage to beg for help did not come until I was 13. I had endured so much abuse that I thought it would be my end if I stayed with him. A rage began to awaken in me that was frightening. It was also at this age when I was molested by him...again. How could I love myself when I was so ashamed of what happened to me? This was not the first time he molested me. When I was two, he took me to his basement where he convinced me that he was going to put a hot dog in my mouth, covered my face with a towel, and put his penis there instead. I repressed everything that happened afterward. I was molested such that I needed to rub a towel against my private area to recreate a sensation I did not understand. I was ashamed that I had these urges. I internalized it all. How could I love myself when no one loved me enough to protect me from this type of abuse?

How was I to love myself when my grandmother witnessed what I was doing, was told about it from daycare providers, recognized the signs of molestation and did not explain to me what was happening and did not fight to protect me? How could I love myself when years later, I had some family members tell me that I was a liar and others that never even asked what happened to me while in his care? How could I love myself when everything I ever experienced was the opposite of love?

Stars & Moons

As I grew older, I harnessed the notion that the way you showed yourself, love, was from the outside in. I was taught by the women around me that if you look good on the outside, you don't have to worry about what you look like on the inside. I learned from most of my immediate family members that the best way to deal with pain was to numb it with alcohol, drugs and/or violence. Where was I to learn how to love myself the right way? I was taught the lie in the church that I was unworthy and undeserving of God's love unless I loved Jesus; a White Man, as depicted on my grandmother's walls, from the Middle East, **(a big question mark for me),** that I did not know. If God did not love me, then how was I to love myself?

Many of us are struggling with what it looks like to truly love ourselves. It wasn't until my early thirties that I began the journey of learning what it truly meant to love myself. I was an alcoholic, which took the form of binge drinking, between the ages of 19 and 25, and then off and on after my son's birth until I was 33. I was in deep credit card debt because I was used to covering up my pain with "things" but could never fill the void. Despite these toxic behaviors, I was highly successful professionally and had earned numerous accolades and awards because another thing I was addicted to was an accomplishment. I was searching for the validation I was never given from the people most important in my life growing up. I was running from my history and my vehicle was an accomplishment.

92

It kept me so busy focusing on work that I did not have the time to sit idle and process all that happened to me as a child.

It wasn't until the accomplishments didn't feel the same anymore that I began to question what I was really after. Validation from others no longer held weight because the only person whose validation mattered had never given it. That person was me. I was so busy accomplishing for other people that I didn't take the time to check in with myself to see what fulfilled me. I was tired of running, tired of empty accolades, tired of being busy to avoid introspection. I wanted to be authentically happy, so I began to seek out self-help, self-realization, and mindset resources. I began to read articles and listen to podcasts from the perspective of successful individuals that started out like me, who were doing the work to unpack and analyze their survival-based belief systems.

I realized that the person I needed to be to survive was different from the person I was to evolve into to thrive. They say "New level. New you.", and it's so true. I realized getting to a place of authenticity would mean taking the time to look at my bad habits and the dark and ugly places within me; it would mean taking care of myself physically, mentally and spiritually.

Mastering Your Universe

I learned that not everyone around you is wrong about you. The people that love you in all of your forms have been telling you about your toxic behavior for years. In my case, my husband consistently told me my communication was horrible. I was so used to being on my own and having to take care of myself that I would do what I wanted with money without involving him, which affected us both especially since I had poor financial habits. I would go out with my friends and not call to check in until I was almost home, while he waited up worrying. Why? I didn't think it was necessary. I knew I was okay and wasn't being unfaithful or anything and that was all that mattered. I was selfish, self-centered and had "Independent Woman" syndrome.

It wasn't until I began this journey of introspection that I realized I never truly allowed him to be "The Man" in my life. Could I live without him? Yes. Did I want to? No. So, why didn't I consider how he felt about my flaws more often? Well, because doing so would force me to look at where those toxic behaviors started. I would need to begin to process my lack of relationship with my father and the tumultuous relationship with my uncle. I would have to come to terms with the fact I had trust and abandonment issues and had a lot of forgiveness work. In other words, I had to *let that shit go*. I would have to admit that I was not always right and that there were other ways to do things other than "My Way". I began to love myself enough to know that I was wrong while reminding myself to be gentle, knowing up until that point, I did the best I knew how.

Up until this point, you have done the best you knew how. Now that you know better, it's time to do better. That is how you fall in love with yourself, by seeing what needs to be constructed in your universe. Fall in love with the prospect of continuous healing and reconstruction. You accept yourself for who you are right now. The parts you like and the parts you don't and know that you are worthy of love just as you are. Show yourself compassion as you dig through your baggage; you will find some pretty nasty things in that bag. Discard them and only keep the things that support where you are trying to go.

Journal Reflections:

To start the rebuilding process of loving yourself. Start to make lists and review them daily to monitor how you are feeding yourself love and vibrational elevation.

◊ List 20 things that you like about yourself.

◊ List 10 things you'd like to change about yourself. How will you go about it? (Do you need to change them? Who said so?)

◊ Draw two columns, one labeled "Helping My Growth" and the other "Hindering My Growth". In the corresponding column, list the things you are doing to support or hinder your growth.

◊ What do you spend the majority of your time doing?

◊ Where do you invest the majority of your energy (social media, watching tv, other people's emergencies, etc.)? Is it helping you to heal or grow?

◊ What are some things you can begin to do to embrace and love on yourself?

MIRROR, MIRROR

"I'm ashamed of the shadow I used to be.

Blending in enough to stay undercover,

standing out enough to do my soul justice.

When you look in the mirror what do you see?

The lie, their reflection of you,

or the truth of who you are and want to be?

I'm not pure, but I am not unclean

I'm not pure, but I am not unclean

I'm not pure, but I am not unclean

Your eyes are your mirror

Be what your soul is reflecting."

(*Mirror by* CB Fletcher)

=======

I've been told that everyone I encounter is a reflection of myself in some way or at least those I spend the most time with (voluntarily or involuntarily). I thought that concept to be asinine because there were people that I found myself around regularly that I would consider being annoying, incompetent, or insufferable. How could they possibly be a reflection of me? I was successful, well-rounded, level-headed, and thriving.

A few years ago, I began to see the same type of person repeatedly and it forced me to take inventory of the people surrounding me professionally. There is a saying:

"If you are the common denominator in every negative situation, _it's you_, not them."

It wasn't until I started my journey of introspection that I reconciled with the fact that I was attracting these types of people because they were a reflection of my unresolved issues personified. If I was dealing with insecurities I was attracted to highly insecure people. If I was dealing with abandonment or inadequacies in relationships, I attracted people who were incredibly needy for my attention and felt insecure about me spending time with other people. Whatever was unresolved within my soul kept reappearing as my reflection until I dealt with it.

There is something called *The Law of Attraction* which has been described as our ability to attract into our lives that which we think about the most. It uses the power of the mind to translate whatever is in our thoughts and materialize them into reality or in other words: **Thoughts become things**. Although the term "Law of Attraction" is fairly recent[1], the concept has been expressed in African and indigenous spiritual teachings for thousands of years as African Culture/spirituality does not separate the mind, body, and spirit as does the

---

[1] 1877 by Russian Occultist, Helen Blavatsky. *Isis Unveiled,* Theosophical University Press, pg. 340

Western World (European influenced/colonized countries).

Although some scientists call The Law of Attraction "pseudoscience", science also teaches us about the power of the mind and its role in healing in medical studies that include a Placebo Group. Oftentimes, people that believe they are receiving medicine to cure their ailment begin to show signs of healing, although they were given a placebo (or sugar pill), reinforcing the saying *"Mind over matter"*. The mind is powerful. It powers our entire body. It propels us into action or keeps us inactive. Therefore, through the energy we radiate (thoughts) and our subsequent actions, our thoughts are brought to life; thus, how we feel about ourselves or unresolved traumas will "bubble up" and manifest within the people and circumstances we attract.

Our subconscious thoughts rule our conscious actions. Sigmund Freud's psychoanalytic theory believed that the conscious, subconscious, and unconscious mind influences our reality[2]. If situations from your childhood made you believe you were unworthy and undeserving, there's a very good chance you internalized these messages and have spent a lifetime reinforcing their validity, subconsciously and unconsciously, through your daily actions.

If you allow fear to infest your subconscious mind, you will manifest the very things you fear. I am seeing this play out more and more as I become aware of how it plays out in my life. For so long, I sought external validation and wondered why I never received it in the way I wanted no matter how much I accomplished. I didn't realize at the time that I wasn't getting the external validation I wanted because I had never given it to myself first and I didn't give myself validation because, subconsciously, I didn't believe I was worthy of it. My subconscious ruled my actions and my actions

---

[2] Journal Psyche. *Freud's Model of the Human Mind 2018.* www.journalpsyche.org

produced more of what I didn't want which were people, places, and things that reinforced I was unworthy, incompetent, and undeserving of abundance and acceptance.

Ask yourself:

1. Do the people, places, and things you are attracting in your life support your growth, or do they encourage your stagnation?

2. What, if anything, does this say about your inner conversations about yourself and your worth?

You can't acknowledge **The Law of Attraction** without also acknowledging the concept of **Projection**. *"Projection is a form of defense in which unwanted feelings are displaced onto another person, where they then appear as a threat from the external world. A common form of projection occurs when an* *individual, threatened by his own angry feelings, accuses another of harboring hostile thoughts.*"[3]

Others project onto us, too. Ever encounter someone that you do not know but treats you unkind? Or have you ever had someone tell you after they have gotten the chance to know you better, that initially, they didn't like you because you reminded them of someone they did not like or trust? It happens all the time because projection is a part of human nature. Psychoanalysts consider projection as one of many human defense mechanisms.

Author of chaos: Sometimes, when we call someone and they don't call us back when we'd like them to, we make up a story that angers us further about why they didn't call us back. I don't know about you but, I've made up entire trilogies about why someone hasn't called, emailed, or texted me back only to find out later that the reason had absolutely nothing to do with me or my trilogy. In

---

[3] The Editors of Encyclopedia Britannica. "Defense Mechanism", Encyclopedia Britannica, Inc., 31 Jan. 2020, www.britannica.com/topic/defense-mechanism

those moments, I am projecting my insecurities and what *I* would be thinking if *I* were them onto them.

Author of hypocrisy: Whenever I encountered someone who I did not care for or who did something I did not care for; I asked the question "Who have I done this to or who am I doing this to currently?" To my surprise, I was subconsciously triggered because I had done the same thing to someone else at one time or another. Sometimes we can be the biggest hypocrites. We get upset with other people for the same things we do to other people.

For example, one of my pet peeves is when someone says they are going to do something, and they don't do it, or they change up how they said they would do it at the last minute. That sends me a message that I am not important, and I cannot trust the person that didn't follow through. This bothers me so much that I often find myself developing a "Plan B" before I even ask someone to do something because I don't trust if they will follow through.

This behavior triggers me so much because when I was a child my caregivers made many promises they did not keep that often left me feeling worthless and embarrassed.

Author of self-compassion: Only after I was able objectively to analyze my behavior, I realized that I do that to other people often. I did that on many occasions with my husband. I would tell him I'd be home from an outing at a certain time, only to overshoot the time by an hour or more without notifying him until the last minute. I would find myself promising things by a certain date, only to provide it after the deadline. I would promise to follow up with someone and fail to do so. I was sending the same message, that I didn't like being given, to people who I cared for tremendously. I was making them feel the same way my caregivers made me feel when they did not keep their word to me: worthless, embarrassed, and unimportant. I realized I had a problem with keeping my word. I was triggered by others that did not keep their word because I did not keep mine.

I still have instances when I mess up and give a word that I do not keep, but now I acknowledge it for what it is and do not become defensive when I'm called on it. One of the ways I circumvent creating a situation where that bad habit may surface is to practice saying "No." I used to have a problem with saying "No" and would agree to do things that I knew I did not want to do or that would deplete my energy (a people-pleasing behavior to avoid rejection and abandonment). Now, if it doesn't align with my values or threatens to deplete my energy or my well-being, I have no problem with saying "No", without explanation. I also better understand the importance and power of my communication. There will be times when a situation changes in a way that affects how and when I said I was going to do something. In those instances, renegotiating and/or giving a heads up that things have changed and requesting accommodations when needed, go a long way. Things change; it's the only thing that is constant but, it's how you govern yourself during these changes that will show others (and yourself) who you truly are.

"No one can make you feel inferior without your consent." – Eleanor Roosevelt

Be gentle with yourself. You can recognize when you're about to project onto others and shift before or while you are doing it. You also can recognize when others are projecting onto you, name it for what it is, and let it bounce right off of you. There have been **several** times I've allowed someone else's projection to lower my energy while I was trying to justify why I wasn't whatever they were trying to say I was. It's exhausting! Now, I can see it for what it is and can either move around it unbothered or quickly recover from the urge to defend myself. I know who I am, and it isn't important to me if others are determined to see me through their distorted lens of projection.

The alluring healing light

Wounded people are attracted to those who have a healing aura about them. When the wounded person latches onto the healing aura they find ways to chip away their light and take it as their own. They do this to imitate the light of that person and fill their wounded void and not work out their issues. Essentially, they want 'the healer' to fix it and leave the healer empty without regard. The healer allows it because of what they see in the wounded person, which is in direct correlation with inadequacies in past relationships with people very close to them. They think or choose to believe:

I Can Save Them

I have been told that I have a healing quality. My interactions with most people are warm and have been likened to being of light. I have experienced "energy leeches" or people that are drawn to such qualities as a moth to a flame. Many of these people have been wounded in their way and were consciously or subconsciously seeking healing and

109

we made a connection immediately for several reasons. One reason is that I am also wounded and until I realized how to access healing from going within, I, too, was seeking healing externally. Ever heard the saying, "looking for love in all the wrong places"? I made the connection with wounded people because I was wounded and thought I would find healing by healing them. *Read that again.*

What I had to realize, though, is not all wounded people are seeking healing. Some of them are seeking to latch on and deplete you of your light because they don't realize they are wounded and in need of healing and it is easier to take your light than to generate their own. How successful they are in leeching your energy will be determined by the boundaries you've set for yourself and your knowledge of self. Your knowledge of self includes understanding your baggage, where it comes from, and how it influences everything you do and every interaction you have. If you are aware of your "stuff", it cannot be used against you.

"When there is no enemy within, the enemies outside cannot hurt you." – African Proverb

Another reason I was allowing Energy Leeches or Wounded People around me was because of my fear of rejection and abandonment. I needed to be liked so people wouldn't leave or abandon me. It was a survival mechanism that no longer served me. Energy Leeches thrive in relationships and situations where they are coddled and fed despite their failure to provide anything of value. In certain situations, seeing the potential in people is not enough to grant them access to your space unchecked. You deserve to experience people whose vibrations elevate you instead of depleting you.

Journal Reflections:

◊ Why do you allow people that are not a vibrational match with you, around you?

◊ What are you trying to prove? Why? To whom?

◊ What types of boundaries or protection do you need to (or have) set for yourself?

◊ How do you want people to treat you?

◊ Does the way you treat yourself and others reflect how you want to be treated?

◊ If not, what are some things you can begin to do to shift this?

YOU ARE WHAT YOU CONSUME

Watch what you consume. This means food, drink, information, and energy.

I had to come to terms with the fact that I had an unhealthy relationship with alcohol, but that wasn't enough. I had to identify healthier things to do when I felt the urge to drink. When I felt triggered and wanted to drown it out with alcohol, instead, I would meditate, write in my journal, exercise or do some other activity that was in line with who I wanted to become. I would remind myself of how horrible I felt when I woke up hung-over and how much I was like my grandmother when she was drinking. I remember how that made me feel as a child when she became belligerent and nasty and I no longer wanted to subject my husband to that.

Consuming coping mechanisms: At one point, my husband and I decided to do a 30-day detox. We each agreed to detox things that were hindering our specific journey towards growth and reflection. I detoxed alcohol, coffee, and high fructose sugars. Once these things were out of my system, I realized that I was trying to drown my anxieties. Up until that point, I had drastically decreased the amount of alcohol I consumed but I would still drink (sometimes heavily) at social gatherings. I would also drink obscene amounts of coffee to give me a jolt of productivity, but it was also a mechanism to deal with my anxiety and was destroying my stomach lining. I have never been a huge fan of sweets, but I began to notice my body's reaction to certain foods that contained high fructose corn syrup. Sugar, especially this type, is known to produce feelings of euphoria and for this reason, it is addictive. I realized I had been using certain foods to counter my feelings of anxiety and worthlessness.

Consuming honesty: I have to be honest, during the 30-Day Detox, I felt like an addict and my husband was my "Sponsor". I would call him while I was out at a social gathering from the coat closet asking if it would be a problem if I had a drink. He would always counter with the question: ***"What***

feeling are you trying to suppress?" When he would ask that question, it would force me to confront the root of my desire to drink. It would also force me to think of other ways I can either embrace or work through the emotion I was feeling.

When I was around a lot of people, especially in professional settings, the mantra that resonated the most was **"I belong here. My presence is of value and a contribution to this space."** When I say those words, the anxiety disappears and I can settle into a mental space where I am comfortable with and confident in who I am, at that moment. I am able to exude authenticity that encourages others to lead with authenticity as well. I have met some of the sincerest, loving, and kind individuals when I have let my guard down and showed up as my authentic self.

Consuming temple maintenance: My husband and I have also begun exploring the vegetarian and vegan lifestyles for many different reasons, with the facts that our bodies don't break down animal proteins and the acknowledgment that most disease is caused by the processed food and meat products we eat. On a journey to align mind, body, and spirit, we cannot ignore the food we consume. What you eat can either bring life and support your mental capacity to connect with Spirit, self, and others or bring death and impede your ability to function. *Your body is your temple.* How are you caring for it? What are you putting into it? How are you healing from the trauma your body has absorbed into its cells? Are you an active participant in your own physical and mental demise?

I am beginning to understand the extent to which my body has been absorbing my trauma over the years. As a child, every time I heard my uncle's voice or heard him waking up on a Saturday morning, I felt nauseous. I didn't know how he was going to wake up feeling and how he felt determined whether or not I would be beaten that day. Almost every day for 8 years, I held fear in my gut and as a 37-year-old woman, I am paying for it. I have made several trips to the Gastroenterologist in hopes of learning where my Irritable Bowel Syndrome symptoms stem from and how to cure them. Now that I understand the connection between my body and my trauma, I am more mindful of what I eat and how food plays a vital role in the rate my body can heal.

Consume reprogramming: The type of information you consume also influences your well-being and physical and emotional growth. What do you spend the majority of your time listening to or viewing? Our subconscious mind is a sponge. As Freud would say, our conscious actions are driven by our subconscious mind. As my belief systems changed, I also began to change what I was watching and listening to. Certain songs that glorified drinking, fighting or drama that I would listen to don't sit right with me anymore. I am embracing the fact that I am an empath. I take on the emotions of other people as if they are my own and I needed to protect my energy, so I stopped watching the news and reality TV and limited time spent with Energy Suckers or eliminated them from my life altogether.

117

I started reading and listening to Self-realization and mindset books. I began to spend my time teaching myself about things I am interested in and connecting with people who are intentional about doing the same thing.

Journal Reflections:

◊ How will you determine how you heal? Write down different things that you consume and journal about how you can set intentions to change it.

◊ What type of spiritual toxins are you consuming?

◊ What type of mental toxins are you consuming?

◊ What type of physical coping mechanisms are you consuming?

◊ What type of things are you watching or engaging in that are not healthy?

◊ What type of dishonesty/excuses about changing your life do you have

MY RELIGION IS LOVE

Namasté

My soul honors your soul.

I honor the place in you where the entire universe resides.

I honor the light, love, truth, beauty, and peace within you, because it is also within me.

In sharing these things, we are united.

We are the same.

We are one.

I was raised as a Baptist. My Godmother, who was my Mother's best friend, took me with her to church almost every Sunday. It didn't matter who I was living with, she made sure we connected in that way. Religion played a major part in my life as a child. I made it a point to read my Bible every day. I looked to God and Jesus to provide an explanation for everything I was experiencing. I needed to know there was a reason for everything I was going through. I had to believe there was something bigger than myself or I would have taken my own life.

There's a terrible lesson that I was taught, and that is not to question God, although, there were so many things that didn't seem to make sense to me related to the religion and related to what was happening in my life and how I was supposed to view my circumstances. I was taught by Christianity that I was unworthy of God's love; it was something I was supposed to earn by repenting or abiding by "His Word". I was taught that God's gender was male; that he was vengeful, jealous and loving. All of which confused me. If we were made in His image, what of women? If He is loving, why is he jealous and vengeful? Love is neither of those things. Why was I given the capacity to think for myself yet told I shouldn't question when my thinking did not add up with what I was being taught in church?

Despite all of these questions and the confusion when I could not get straight answers from people in the church, I still continued to believe in this particular way of exercising my belief in God. I knew of no other way and to go too deep into questioning a way of life that had provided security in the midst of pain and uncertainty was scary to me.

The family I lived with in Georgia was Pentecostal, and I learned very quickly how this particular sect of Christianity differed from the Baptist practices I was so used to. They believed there were demons and angels walking amongst us and often cast demons out at church service. It was a terrifying experience to witness, to say the least. We went to church almost every day of the week and stayed there for hours! I found myself so exhausted between dealing with bullying at school, my uncle leaving me in Georgia with a bag of clothes and nothing else, living with strangers, and living with the expectations of the religion I was now forced to practice.

At each service, part of the program was to "Tarry" (say "Thank You Jesus) until you spoke tongues which was explained to me as being a language that only me and God could understand. Eventually, I got to a point where I was actually speaking tongues. It scared me at first but when I spoke it, I felt like I had a direct connection to something bigger than me. Although I couldn't understand what I was saying, I was told my spirit could. Believing this and constantly being around people that believed in something more than themselves helped me tremendously. It distracted me from my reality.

When I was able to convince my Uncle during one of his brief visits to see me, to let me visit my family back in Baltimore, I was relieved. While I was living with Ms. Sarah, the Uncle that left me there warned that I was not to contact my grandmother, other uncle or cousins to let them know where I was. Although I was living with Ms. Sarah for less than a year, it felt like forever, especially when I wasn't able to connect with any of the family members that I loved so much.

After returning to Baltimore 8 months after living in Georgia, I was able to continue attending church with my Godmother like I was used to and although my questions about God and Jesus were still never properly answered, I was relieved to continue practicing a belief I was familiar with.

I began tithing consistently in my Senior year in high school. I was able to do this as I secured a steady job bagging at the local grocery store. When I enrolled in college and began living on campus, it was more difficult to maintain my tithing payments and as a result, I was no longer considered a member of the church. This upset and confused me because I was at a transition in my life where I needed a lot of support and it made sense to me that my church would want to support me like I had been told to do for them but, that was not reciprocated.

In my sophomore year in college, I became so holier-than-thou that I pushed away many of my friends. I spent my time with them trying to bring them to Christ and disapproving of their worldly behaviors. I even became celibate with my boyfriend of 3 years, without his understanding why, because I didn't want to upset God or Jesus – the people I went to church with seemed to interchange the two, although they were explained to me to have been separate entities.

In my Junior year of college, I began to analyze my beliefs around church and Christianity. When I did this, I realized that I believed what I did for two reasons. The first was I was indoctrinated from birth. I believed and practiced it because everyone around me did. The second reason was because of fear. I was told if I didn't believe or if I questioned Jesus or God, I would go to hell. Hell was described as the scariest place you can envision, and I definitely did not want to end up there with the "gnawing and gnashing of teeth".

Shortly after, I met my husband, Brian. When we began dating, religion was a topic that we discussed and debated often. He was not religious. He considered himself spiritual but agnostic at times.

He would challenge me with questions about my belief system that I could not answer. We would talk about the soul and what we thought it was and how we transcended space and time. I began to realize that the religious beliefs I held onto were not "*the only*" way to the light and that all religions overlap on certain principles on their journey to God or what Buddhist call Nirvana. I decided that, for me, where they overlapped was Truth and everything else stemmed from the human limitations of fear and judgment.

It wasn't until I was in my thirties, when I started my quest of trying to understand myself and the world I lived in through a spiritual lens. It led me down the path of seeking my African Ancestry and everything began to make sense to me. The questions that Christianity could not or would not answer, my African Ancestry and culture could. Not only was I previously practicing the same religion that was used to enslave and control my ancestors, but I was subscribing to a Western belief system that did not honor the Mind, Body and Spirit connection. I was scared into believing my ancestors' beliefs were barbaric and evil when historically more people have been killed in the name of Christianity than almost any other religion.

Spirituality is the connection to the outer and internal spiritual interactions we practice and encounter.

I believe that we are all spiritual beings that choose to honor our spirituality through different religions. Some of us choose not to honor it at all, but I don't believe that takes away from our spirituality. We are all connected to each other and all living things regardless of whether we notice or acknowledge it. I have come to a point in my life where I believe there is more than one path to the light and as long as we are seeking it, without harming others, there is no right or wrong way.

Through meditation and actively seeking information from spiritual teachers, I have begun to see myself as an immense contribution to this world. Even more importantly, I am beginning to see my inner divinity and just how much influence I have over my present and my future.

Growing up in church, I was told that I was not worthy, ridden with sin even if I had done nothing, unlovable and it was only because of God's mercy that I am alive in all of my wretchedness. I was told I was unclean and undeserving. As a child already dealing with abandonment, rejection and abuse, this belief did more to hurt me than inspire or nurture me. As an adult working through my baggage, I realize this religious perspective is not for me because it is not true.

I believe we all are born divine beings as we are all manifestations of God's consciousness and reflections of its love. How we take on the task to be reflections of God's love is entirely dependent on the person's ego and the level of surrender to anointed guidance. The true religion is Love and anything built on fear and ignorance is not of God.

I have had people tell me that the only way my marriage will work is if I am a Christian. People have told me that the only way to be an honorable example of a woman to my son is to be a Christian. Folks have told me that I will not be blessed if I do not consider myself a Christian. I have been told that if I do not believe the way Christians do, I will burn in hell. That's absurd, especially since Christians can get divorced, give up or abandon their children, and fall on hard times like everyone else. Also, there are people who don't consider themselves Christians that lead happy, fulfilling, and blessed lives full of love as the promise of Christianity says. Ultimately it comes down to how the person operates with or without faith. Reading scripture about how *to love thy neighbor* are simple words if you spend your time attacking people who don't look, believe, think, or have the same finances as you.

I've also heard of Christians that do not believe any of those things but by virtue of being a Christian and following the Bible, they must believe that all people that do not believe or follow Jesus Christ are destined for hell. This belief does not sit right in my spirit and is one of the many reasons why I decided to challenge my own set of beliefs. *I do not regret any of my religious experiences.* They have built the foundation for what I believe today. My decision to shift my belief system has led me down a path of self-realization, purpose, and a respect for myself, others, and nature that I cannot describe. It is not driven by fear. It is driven and sustained by light and love.

My hope is that you challenge any beliefs you have collected and subscribed to over the years. Revisit them to see if they are still relevant and if they will lead you to the life you've always wanted. Examine all of them. Your beliefs about people, yourself, your religion, your politics, etc. In the information age, there is no excuse to live in ignorance. What worked for us as children, will not work for us as adults. Our goals as children tend to evolve and shift as we grow and so should belief systems that no longer serve us. It takes a brave individual to do this because it is not pleasant. Breaking a habit is almost always difficult until it is done. It is a process but that is what this life is about, learning from and being with the process – your process. Seek Yourself and you will be found.

Journal Reflections:

◊ What have you believed by osmosis and now you question it?

◊ How have you tried to create your own relationship with God (by any name)?

◊ Do you love people as they are or because your faith deems it so?

◊ What has your walk with religion/God taught you about how to handle the turmoil of life?

◊ If you met an atheist or agnostic how would you 'convince' them that there is a God? Would you talk about personal experiences or regurgitate what has been ingrained in you via your faith?

DIVINE WOMANHOOD

"I am a woman, phenomenally. A phenomenal woman, that's me."- Dr. Maya Angelou

Just like the legendary Dr. Maya Angelou, the molestation I experienced as a child impacted my development as a woman. My vision of femininity was distorted. The shame from the molestation coupled with the lack of information shared about my body interfered with my sense of self-worth and fractured my relationship with myself.

In hindsight, the day my grandmother discovered me trying to "self-soothe" as a 4 or 5-year-old, was the day. She was aware of what I was doing and did not scold nor acknowledge what I was doing, I was just told to go to bed. The look in her eyes was a mixture of pain, defeat and familiarity. As a grown woman looking back at that moment, I realize she was witnessing history repeat itself. It makes me wonder who did the same thing to her and how it impacted her life. The shame I was feeling wasn't my own, she shared some of hers with me in that exchange and many thereafter.

She would often tell me how men didn't care about anything but my "*Moochee*". I remember one time when she had been drinking, she called me into the kitchen during one of her tirades, pulled down my underwear, and hit my private area, saying something to the effect that all men want is my "*Moochee*". I was five years old, confused, and embarrassed. I was subconsciously being taught that my vagina was something to be ashamed of and that what men wanted to do with it was something to fear.

Although I believe the term *"Moochee"* was made up, it makes me think of the word from which it is derived, "Moocher" which means *"a person who lives off others without giving anything in return."* Why should my *Womb-manhood* be referred to as something that lives off others without giving anything in return? My womb gives the ultimate gift of life. It makes me wonder who told her this about herself? Who gave her this adjective to describe the most divine thing in creation?

Our understanding of sex and its connection to our physical, mental, and spiritual development are passed on from our elders. Often, the disappointment, shame, and trauma they've experienced in their sexual encounters are passed onto the next generation. I know my grandmother was raped and that her eldest child was a product of it, but I am sure there are so many other traumatic sexual experiences that shaped her relationship with herself and her femininity.

I am learning the power and divinity of my womanhood; It is sacred, it is the portal through which all life comes into this world. Without it, none of us would exist. The power of the womb is so strong that historically men have tried to suppress it for millennia. We are written out of history books, limited and disregarded by religious doctrine, systemically suppressed and fooled into consuming image-destroying propaganda. Double standards shame us into rejecting our sexual desires and well-being while men are celebrated for embracing theirs. The societal discourse around Womanhood combined with my sexual trauma created a disconnect between me, my womb, and my sexual health.

I am still working to unpack all of what this means and to call it out when I see it in action. As I explore my African heritage, I am learning how much my ancestors celebrated masculine and feminine energies equally and how they viewed them as complementary, not in competition to each other. We have been misled into believing that one is better than the other and that we have to choose which one we will be, ignoring the fact that every one of us has both masculine and feminine qualities and even share similar physiology. Knowing this, I have a greater appreciation for how my husband compliments me and a greater appreciation for how both of these energies exist *within* me. I can now strive for balance, giving attention to my femininity and honoring the divinity of my **Womb**-manhood, as I have spent most of my life giving more attention to the masculine attributes associated with being a "Strong and Independent Black Woman". We are all interdependent; no one is truly independent. We need each other to survive and thrive.

Journal Reflections:

◊ How do you empower yourself from your physique to your mind to your soul?

◊ If you have had sexual trauma how have you gotten back in touch with your sexual self and your spiritual self?

◊ What are some ways you can make sure your children or youth, in general, understand their divine selves and physical beings?

◊ How do you define gender roles or do you?

◊ How will you encourage your significant other or spouse to engage in sex in a healthy

way that will heal traumas and become both a
spiritual and pleasurable experience?

THERE IS ALWAYS SOMETHING TO BE GRATEFUL FOR

"Acknowledging the good that you already have in your life is the foundation for all abundance."-

- Eckhart Tolle

As painful as it has been living without my mother and navigating all the issues stemming from having a broken childhood, I wouldn't change a thing. I didn't always feel this way. I used to dream of having a time machine and being able to go back in time to save my mother or convince my father that he should be in my life. I used to resent not having a childhood and the fact that at my most vulnerable, the adults in my life responsible for my care did not protect me. Despite all of that I am eternally grateful for where I am in my life and all that I have.

I look at my life today and realize that it is what I prayed for and more, with one small change it could have altered the path to my purpose; that would be unfulfilling, and my life would be void. Just thinking that one small change could mean that my son, Amani, wouldn't be here or that I wouldn't have met my husband, is heart-wrenching. I have been able to advocate for children in foster care so fiercely and effectively because I was in foster care and I know what it feels like. Without that experience, working in child welfare never would have happened and there would be no impact on the lives I have been able to touch and change. I don't operate in the world of hypotheticals so, the life I have today, is the life I have, and I cannot be more grateful for it.

Practice Gratitude

You hear a lot of people say to practice gratitude in order to attract new things in your life. This is difficult to hear when life has not been kind, so what is there to be grateful for? The lessons. The strengthening. Spiritual evolution. The skills. The list goes on if you allow yourself to see beyond the circumstance. Zoom out from your circumstances and see how this has affected your growth across the board. By doing so you will attract the polar opposite of the things that hurt you and create a new foundation for a positive life.

Make two columns. List things that have hurt you throughout your life in one column and what you learned, gained, replaced after you accepted the lesson or experience, in the other column.

(see next page)

My List

Things that Hurt Me	What I learned/Gained/Replaced
I grew up in abusive situations, so I know what it is like to feel unloved.	I have a intelligent, kind, and funny son that I love with my whole heart and he has never known the sting of not feeling loved.
I did not know the love of my father or have examples of a healthy relationship	I have a supportive, patient, loving husband that showed me how to love and be loved on a soul level
I had to create a "community" in order to survive.	I have close friends and family that I do not have to protect myself from and we thrive, not survive, together.
I had to fight to be noticed for a career and learn how to network without guidance	I manifested skills that have created my own soul-fulfilling lane in the world, and I am able to transform lives whilst being a very committed wife and mother.
I was tormented by some family members who were dealing with their own wounds by unleashing their frustrations on me.	I developed the spiritual fortitude, mental stamina, emotional resolution, and physical peace to never allow the curses of my elders to manifest in me as I raise my son alongside my husband who uplifts our mission to create a new fruitful foundation.

MY HOPE FOR YOU

I hope through the vulnerability of sharing such intimate parts of myself and my story, I have helped you to see your worth and beauty.

I hope you can see power in your own story and vulnerability.

There is nothing you cannot do because everything you need to live your dreams is inside of you.

Abundance in all forms is your birthright but, the person you must convince of this, is yourself.

I hope you find the happiness that is already yours.

I hope you find the courage to break your generational curses.

I hope you heal.

Love,

Muffin